Data Scientist

by India James

BLASTOFF! READERS, AN IMPRINT OF BELLWETHER MEDIA BY FLUTTERBEE

Blastoff! Readers are carefully developed by literacy experts to build reading stamina and move students toward fluency by combining standards-based content with developmentally appropriate text.

LEVELS

Level 1 provides the most support through repetition of high-frequency words, light text, predictable sentence patterns, and strong visual support.

Level 2 offers early readers a bit more challenge through varied sentences, increased text load, and text-supportive special features.

Level 3 advances early-fluent readers toward fluency through increased text load, less reliance on photos, advancing concepts, longer sentences, and more complex special features.

★ **Blastoff! Universe**

Reading Level

Grade K

Grades 1–3

Grade 4

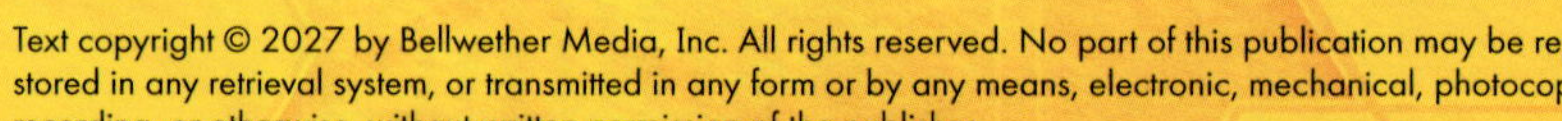

This edition first published in 2027 by Bellwether Media, Inc.

For information regarding permission, write to Bellwether Media, Inc., Attention: Permissions Department, 3500 American Blvd W, Suite 150, Bloomington, MN 55431.

Library of Congress Cataloging-in-Publication Data is available at www.loc.gov or upon request from the publisher.

ISBN: 9798898800765 (hardcover)
ISBN: 9798898802004 (ebook)

Editor: Betsy Rathburn Designer: Andrea Schneider

Printed in the United States of America, North Mankato, MN.

Weather Report 4
What Is a Data Scientist? 6
At Work 10
Becoming a Data Scientist 16
Glossary 22
To Learn More 23
Index 24

Weather Report

Dark clouds fill the sky. Is it going to rain?

A **data** scientist looks at their computer screen. It is filled with **information** about weather. It will be sunny again soon!

What Is a Data Scientist?

Numbers and words are all around us. The world is filled with this data.

Data scientists use it to help make our lives better. Some work for businesses. Others work for the government.

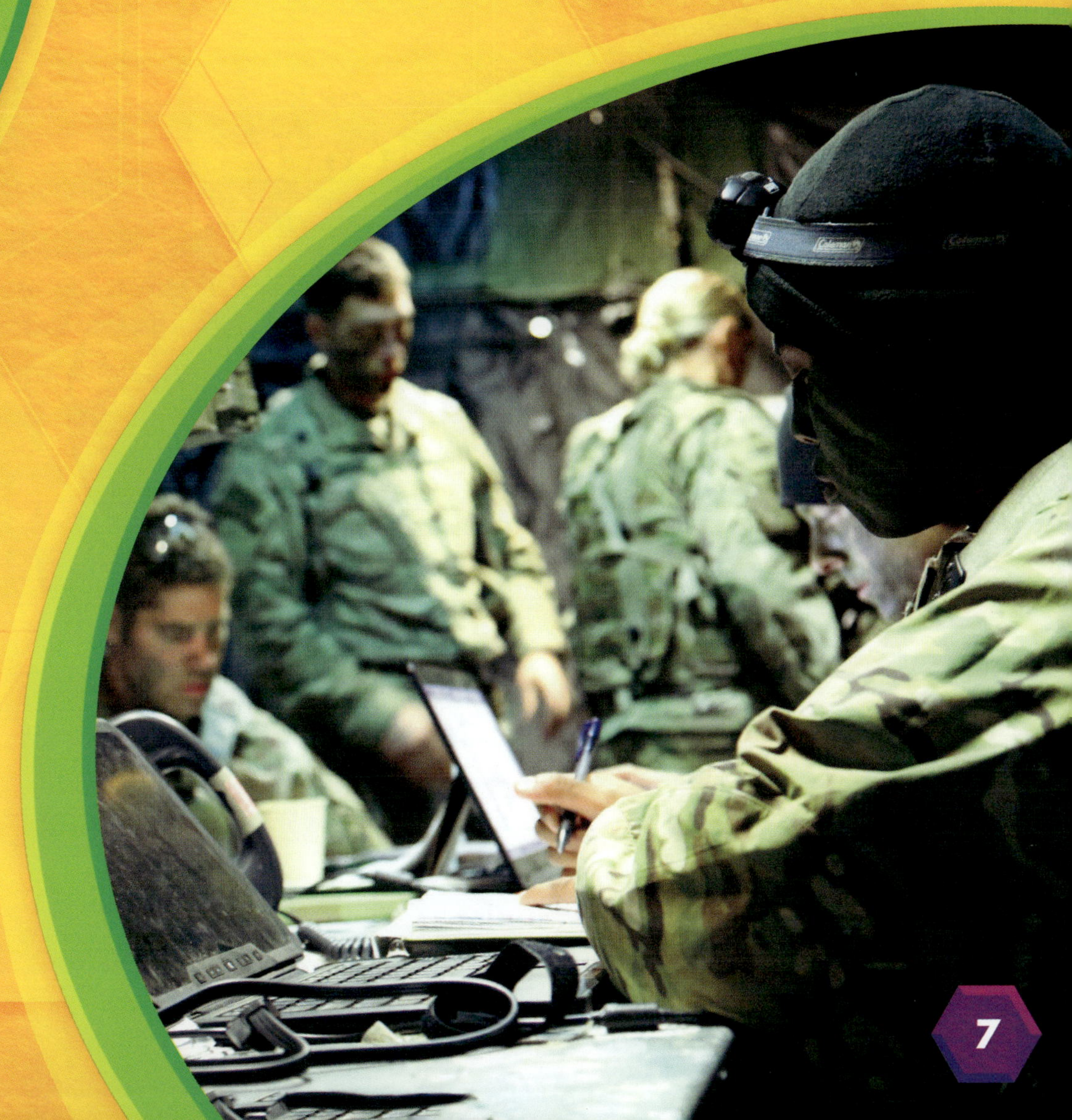

These workers ask questions. They use facts to find answers.

Famous Data Scientist

Name — DJ Patil

Born — August 3, 1974

Birthplace — India

Schooling — University of California, San Diego; University of Maryland, College Park

Known For — used weather data to help predict weather more easily

They help **predict** the weather. They help banks make good decisions. They even work with video games and movies.

At Work

These workers use computers. Some look at what people buy. Some look at what people watch or play.

Others collect data about the world around us. They may look at the weather or the **solar system**.

ask questions and look for answers

Technology

use computers to collect data

make tools to study data

build models using collected data

Data scientists use **programming languages**. They build **models** to study data. They use **artificial intelligence** and **machine learning**.

These tools help them find patterns in data.

programming language

They use what they find to help make decisions. They can tell businesses to make different products.

They can tell people to prepare for bad weather.

Data Science in Real Life

better ideas of what to buy

better weather predictions

better results when searching the internet

Becoming a Data Scientist

Most data scientists go to college. Many study computers. Others study math. **Statistics** is a common subject.

They often learn programming languages. These help them build models.

Every project is different. Data scientists learn a lot for each job they work on.

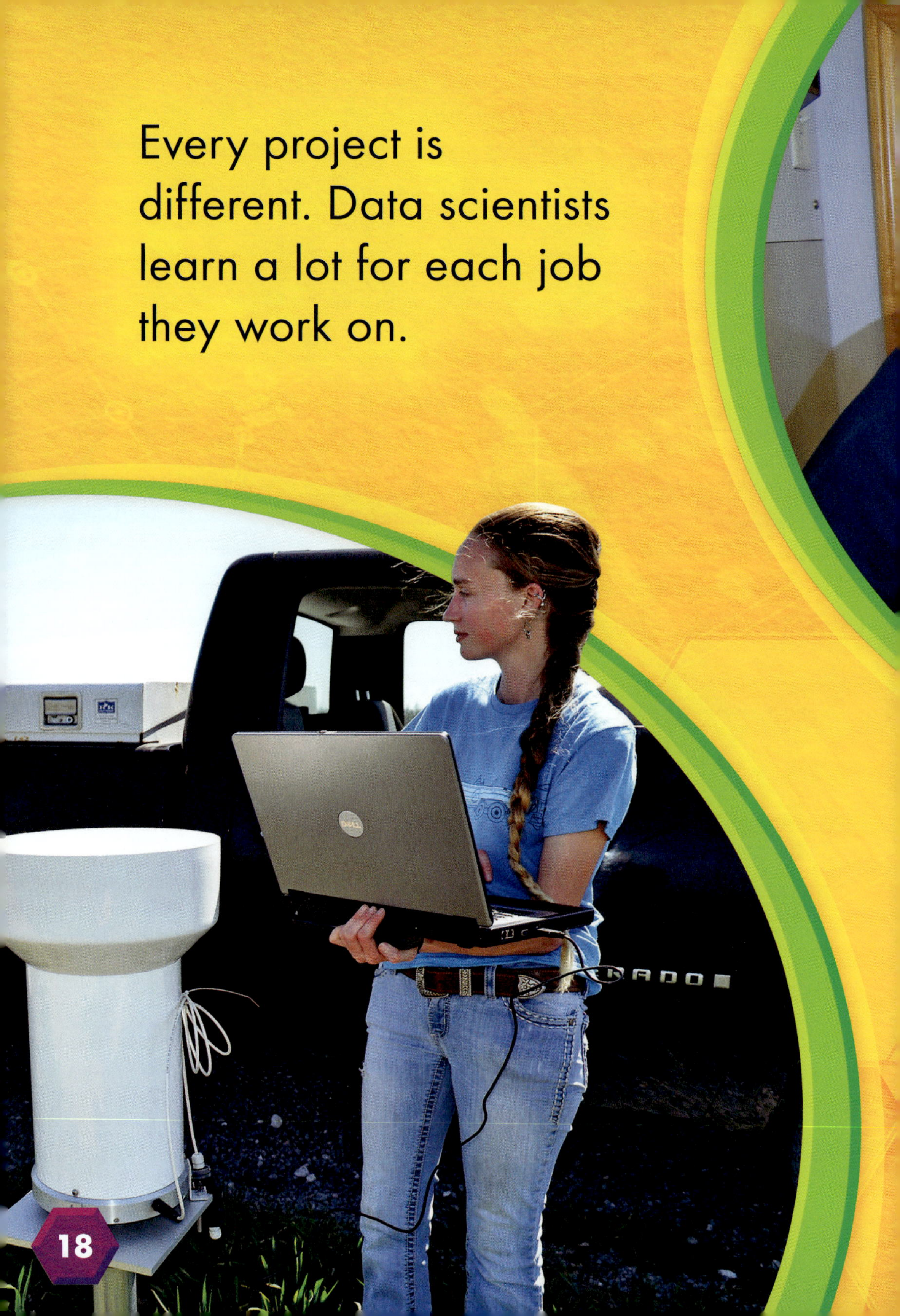

They gain work experience. **Internships** help them. They learn outside of school.

Data scientists keep learning after school is done. They often train for **certificates**. These show that they have certain skills.

How to Become a Data Scientist

1. go to college
2. get experience through internships
3. continue learning on each project

4. gain certificates

This is an important job!

Glossary

artificial intelligence—a computer's ability to do things a human mind can do

certificates—documents that show a person has learned a skill

data—facts and information

information—facts and knowledge

internships—programs in which people work at a job to gain work experience

machine learning—the practice of giving information to computers so that they can learn on their own

models—systems of data used to help make decisions or predictions

predict—to guess based on collected data

programming languages—sets of instructions used to make computer programs

solar system—the group of planets, moons, asteroids, and other bodies that circle around the Sun

statistics—a branch of math that deals with the study of data

To Learn More

AT THE LIBRARY

Bell, Samantha S. *Coding Algorithms*. Minneapolis, Minn.: Abdo, 2024.

Harris, Christopher. *What Is Machine Learning?* Buffalo, N.Y.: PowerKids Press, 2025.

Spiro, Ruth. *How To Explain Coding To A Grown-Up*. Watertown, Mass.: Charlesbridge, 2023.

ON THE WEB

FACTSURFER

Factsurfer.com gives you a safe, fun way to find more information.

1. Go to www.factsurfer.com.
2. Enter "data scientist" into the search box and click 🔍.
3. Select your book cover to see a list of related content.

Index

artificial intelligence, 12
businesses, 7, 14
certificates, 20
college, 16, 19, 20
data science in real life, 15
famous data scientist, 8
government, 7
how to become, 20
internships, 19
models, 12, 16
programming languages, 12, 16
using STEM, 11
weather, 4, 9, 11, 15

The images in this book are reproduced through the courtesy of: Blue Jean Images/ Alamy, front cover (data scientist); nerminmuminovic, front cover (servers); hasanstudio, p. 3; liubovsolo, p. 4 (inset); AndreyPopov, pp. 4-5; Gorodenkoff, pp. 6-7; BillionPhotos.com, p. 6 (data); U.S. Army JMRC by Spc. Hayden Allega/ Wikipedia, p. 7; Christopher Michel/ Wikipedia, p. 8 (Patil); Ryan McGinnis/ Alamy, pp. 8-9; The National Guard/ Wikipedia, pp. 10-11; NOIRLab/ NSF/ AURA/ R. Sparks & P. Marenfeld/ Wikipedia, p. 10 (inset); matejmo, p. 12 (programming language); Dean Calma/ IAEA/ Wikipedia, pp. 12-13; DragonImages/ Alamy, pp. 14-15; Kittiphat, p. 15 (what to buy); US National Weather Service/ Wikipedia, p. 15 (weather predictions); Internet Archive/ Wikipedia, p. 15 (internet); Worawee Meepian, p. 16 (inset); JFarbarik/ Wikipedia, pp. 16-17; Science History Images/ Alamy, p. 18 (bottom); USEPA Environmental-Protection-Agency/ Wikipedia, pp. 18-19; Asier, pp. 20-21 (data scientist); U.S. Navy photo by John F. Williams/ Wikipedia, pp. 20-21 (top); Sefo, p. 23.